The Wonder of
BUTTERFLIES

For a free color catalog describing Gareth Stevens Publishing's list of high-quality books and multimedia programs, call 1-800-542-2595 (USA) or 1-800-461-9120 (Canada). Gareth Stevens Publishing's Fax: (414) 332-3567.

Library of Congress Cataloging-in-Publication Data

Bauman, Amy.
    The wonder of butterflies / by Amy Bauman and E. Jaediker Norsgaard;
  illustrated by John F. McGee.
      p. cm. — (Animal wonders)
    Summary: Text and photographs introduce these creatures whose
  life cycles span the changes from egg to adult butterfly.
    ISBN 0-8368-2662-0 (lib. bdg.)
    1. Butterflies—Juvenile literature. [1. Butterflies.] I. Norsgaard, E. Jaediker
  (Ernestine Jaediker). II. McGee, John F., ill. III. Title. IV. Series.
  QL544.2.B4   2000
  595.78'9—dc21   00-039515

First published in North America in 2000 by
Gareth Stevens Publishing
A World Almanac Education Group Company
330 West Olive Street, Suite 100
Milwaukee, WI 53212 USA

This edition is based on the book *Butterflies for Kids* © 1996 by E. Jaediker Norsgaard, with illustrations by John F. McGee, first published in the United States in 1996 by NorthWord Press, Inc., Minocqua, Wisconsin, and published as *Butterfly Magic for Kids* in a library edition by Gareth Stevens, Inc., in 1996. Additional end matter © 2000 by Gareth Stevens, Inc.

Photographs © 1996: Sharon Cummings/Dembinsky Photo Associates: Cover, 7, 10, 31, 40; Skip Moody/ Dembinsky Photo Associates: 28, 32, 39; Gary Meszaros/Dembinsky Photo Associates: 8, 29; Rod Planck/Dembinsky Photo Associates: 17, 18, 38, 45; John Gerlach/Dembinsky Photo Associates: 25; Jim Brandenburg/Minden Pictures: 6, 34, 41; Frans Lanting/Minden Pictures: 24, 33; Frank Oberle: 43; John Shaw: 16, 20, 22, 23, 44; Richard Hamilton Smith: 12-13; Clay Myers/The Wildlife Collection: 27.

Printed in the United States of America

1 2 3 4 5 6 7 8 9 04 03 02 01 00

The Wonder of
BUTTERFLIES

by Amy Bauman and E. Jaediker Norsgaard
Illustrations by John F. McGee

Gareth Stevens Publishing
A WORLD ALMANAC EDUCATION GROUP COMPANY

In summer, colorful flowers are in full bloom. Where flowers grow, you will also find beautiful butterflies!

There are many types of butterflies. Each type has a certain place to live and grow and favorite foods to eat.

butterfly egg next to a coin

Every butterfly begins its life as a tiny egg. A creature called a larva hatches from the egg. Another name for the larva is *caterpillar*.

monarch butterfly

red admiral butterfly

Caterpillars are very fussy about which plants they eat! Butterflies lay their eggs on plants they know the caterpillars will eat.

Some
caterpillars
use plants
for shelter,
too. They
pull the
leaves of
a plant
around
themselves
and keep
the leaves
closed with
sticky silk.

Although female butterflies might lay hundreds of eggs, they will lay only one egg on each leaf.

buckeye butterfly

Monarch butterflies lay eggs on the leaves of milkweed plants. After laying their eggs, butterflies leave. They do not stay to take care of the eggs.

Monarchs also drink nectar from milkweed plants. This nectar makes the monarchs taste bad to predators. Their bad taste protects them from birds and other insects looking for food. Hardly any animal wants to eat a monarch!

monarch butterfly

All butterflies go through four stages of growth to change from an egg into an adult. These changes are called metamorphosis. If you look closely at a butterfly egg, you might see a black dot. This dot is the head of a butterfly larva — a caterpillar.

Caterpillars grow fast. As they grow, they shed their skin, or molt, many times.

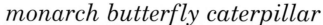
monarch butterfly caterpillar

Caterpillars spend most of their time eating and growing.

Besides molting, the wormlike larva goes through other changes before it becomes a beautiful butterfly.

comma butterfly

The next change is the pupa stage. During this stage, a full-grown caterpillar begins to form a butterfly body.

American copper butterfly

As a pupa, the caterpillar rests. Although it seems to be doing nothing, it is very busy growing. An outer shell called a chrysalis protects the pupa in this resting stage.

monarch butterfly

Becoming a pupa is hard work for a caterpillar. To begin, the caterpillar must find a special spot to make its chrysalis.

Some caterpillars choose
a spot on a branch or
a plant stalk.
Most will
hang upside
down at
this spot.
They hang
by their
two back
legs, which are
attached to the branch
or stalk with silk.

monarch butterfly caterpillar

The caterpillar then sheds its skin one last time. It wriggles and stretches until the skin comes off.

At first, the pupa is just a soft blob, but it quickly forms a hard, smooth shell — the chrysalis.

monarch butterfly pupa

monarch butterfly chrysalises

Over time, the creature inside the chrysalis grows and changes into an adult butterfly.

To survive through all their stages of growth, both caterpillars and butterflies have to protect themselves from danger. Caterpillars and butterflies have many predators.

great spangled fritillary butterfly

Some caterpillars scare away their enemies with a bad smell or prickly hair. Some have spots that look like eyes.

tiger swallowtail butterfly caterpillar

black swallowtail butterfly

Some butterflies also have eyespots to frighten away enemies. Black swallowtail butterflies have one eyespot on each of their back wings.

Spicebush swallowtail butterflies do not have eye-spots on their wings. They do, however, have eyespots during their caterpillar stage.

spicebush swallowtail butterfly

In the pupa stage, swallowtail caterpillars do not hang upside down. Instead, they attach their hind legs to a branch or plant stalk and stand straight up.

They weave
a "safety
belt" of silk
around
their bodies.
The silk
holds them
securely to
the branch
or stalk.

*black swallowtail
butterfly pupa*

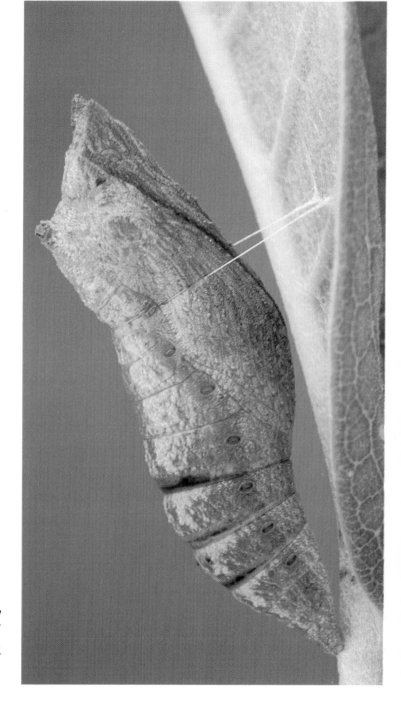

When a butterfly is ready to come out of its shell, the chrysalis starts to change colors. Finally, the butterfly's wings show through the chrysalis.

monarch butterfly chrysalis

Then, the chrysalis splits open. The new butterfly clings to the empty shell with its legs. It must wait for its wings to dry before it can fly.

new monarch butterfly

monarch butterfly wing

All butterflies have four wings — two wings on each side. The wings are made of tiny scales that overlap.

A butterfly has a small, coiled tube instead of a mouth. This tube is called a proboscis. The butterfly drinks nectar from flowers through its proboscis.

Some butterflies migrate long distances. In fall, many monarchs fly south. They can travel thousands of miles, from the northern regions of North America to Florida, California, and Mexico.

painted lady butterfly

About 20,000 species, or types, of butterflies live in our world.

The American painted
lady butterfly is also called
"hunter's butterfly." It has
two eyespots under each
of its back wings.

American painted lady butterfly

viceroy butterfly

Viceroy butterflies look a lot like the bad-tasting monarchs — predators won't eat them, either!

monarch butterflies

With their wings open,
the biggest butterflies are
almost 1 foot (0.3 meters)
across. Black swallowtails
have a wingspan of about
3 inches (8 centimeters).

black swallowtail butterfly

checkered skipper butterfly

Most skipper butterflies
are medium-sized, with
thick, mothlike bodies.

Pearl crescents are tiny butterflies. Their wingspan is less than 1.5 inches (4 cm).

pearl crescent butterfly

From egg to adult, butterflies go through amazing changes during their lives!

In all their shapes, sizes, and colors, these elegant creatures add beauty and wonder to our world.

Glossary

larva – the young, wingless form of an insect that hatches from an egg

metamorphosis – a change in appearance or form. In butterflies, this process includes four stages — egg, larva, pupa, and adult.

migrate – regularly travel to a different region

molts – sheds hair, feathers, shells, or other outer layers and grows new ones

moth – an insect with wings that is related to the butterfly. Unlike most butterflies, moths are dull in color and have plump, fuzzy bodies.

predators – animals that hunt other animals for food

proboscis – a long, flexible, strawlike tube. In butterflies, the proboscis acts as a mouth.

pupa – the stage of growth during which a caterpillar changes into a butterfly

Index